# *Love* Poems

By: Robert Eaton Sokol

Copyright © 2019 by Robert Eaton Sokol

ISBN-13: 978-1-61957-002-3
ISBN-10: 1-61957-002-5

BISAC: Language Arts & Disciplines

Poetry All rights reserved.

No part of this book may be reproduced or transmitted in any form or by any means, electronic or mechanical, including photocopying, recording, or by any information storage and retrieval system, without permission in writing from the copyright owner.

This book was printed in the United States of America.

Okab Publishing, LLC
P.O. Box 79029
Charlotte, NC 28271

## *Dedication*

I dedicate this and all my writings to:

My parents, Oscar and Frances Sokol, who hired a tutor when I was 16. I could not read well and had very poor reading comprehension. I had almost no recollection of anything I did read. She taught me words and word meanings so at least I could start. They then sent me to a special school so I could learn. My high school English Teacher, Mrs. Martha Crowley, taught me how to focus because my eyes fluttered when I attempted to focus. She had an amazing speed-reading machine that did this. I was not dumb and trying harder was not my problem. I simply could not "see word order."

My beloved wife, Dorothy, who constantly encourages me to write even more, to expand my already expansive imagination to greater heights. I am a Heart Poet. I write from my Heart perspective first, then my mind. If I do not feel it, I do not write it. But when I do, words flow effortlessly and with love. .

# *Preface*

Poetry is a suggestive art Using symbols and direct imitation of Life, it stimulates the imagination of the reader through imagery, taking strong hold of their feelings, arousing them to passionate reaction. It also appeals to understanding, and is, therefore, capable of directing lessons of wisdom.

Poetry is the spontaneous overflow of powerful feelings, recollected in tranquility. It reflects the beauty of thought, of feeling, of expression and technical skill. It should be an outlet for one's own unspoken thoughts and varied moods. It makes articulate, our inadequate speech giving adequate expression to our static, yet kinetic loves, joys, glories, furnishing release and relief of one's fears, grief and sorrows.

A poet's job is to salute the mind by creating imagery through the senses; the nose, the ears, sight, touch and taste, creating memories of moments past and views of the present. It is this task, recounting for our senses and experiences, without doubt and in as few words as possible that accurately describe the experience and/ or view of life.

# Table of Contents

| | |
|---|---|
| A Love to Remember | 1 |
| A Mother's Rain | 3 |
| And so, It Goes to my Toes | 4 |
| Baby, It's Cold Outside, But Warm In Your Heart! | 5 |
| Between You And Me | 6 |
| Black Is Cool and Powered by Joy | 8 |
| Curious Mind and Ruby Red Lips | 10 |
| Discover the Beginning | 11 |
| Fire Flies, Twinkling Stars and Goose Bumps | 12 |
| Fishing for Goodness | 14 |
| Found Love | 15 |
| Gift | 16 |
| How Do I Know | 17 |
| Gratitude and Thankfullness | 19 |
| Happy Dance | 20 |
| Real Joy, Strength and Courage | 22 |
| Is Born from Love | 22 |
| How Do I Know? | 24 |
| How Do I Love You & Butterfly Kisses? | 26 |
| How Long Are Your Fingers? Let's Have Diner. | 27 |
| How Will I Find You? | 28 |
| I Am High On Feeling | 29 |
| I am an Idea in the Mind of God and I am Here. | 31 |
| I Am The Lucky One, But It Is Not Luck At All | 32 |
| I Thought about You! | 34 |
| If Only I Could Be Forever | 35 |
| Inspiration: | 37 |
| The Beginning, The Middle, The End | 38 |
| It Was In November When We Met. | 39 |
| Its Not Always As It Seems, Or Is It? | 40 |
| Pink is my Favorite Color | 41 |

| | |
|---|---|
| Just A Little Bit, Can Make Me Do Great Things | 42 |
| Kings And Queens: Would-Be | 43 |
| Let's Dance! | 44 |
| Life Statement: It Is All Good And It Is God. | 45 |
| I Am An Idea In The Mind Of God And I Am There. | 46 |
| Listen | 47 |
| My Addiction Is Love and Significance | 49 |
| My Best Friend, My Love, How I See Thee | 51 |
| My Goddess, She Lives With-In Me. | 53 |
| It's My Heart, Not A Burp Left From Your Hurt | 54 |
| My Ride With Destiny | 55 |
| New Choices Today | 56 |
| Not Just Any Goddess | 57 |
| Our Love Is Here To Stay | 58 |
| Partnership: A Process | 59 |
| Pieaou: A Special Flavoring Born Of Love. | 61 |
| Please Wait For Me, I Will Be There Soon. | 62 |
| Poetry In Motion | 64 |
| Self Worth And Value | 65 |
| She Walked In | 67 |
| So Much In Love, It's More Than Titles For Right Living | 68 |
| Soft Rain Or Delicate Snow | 69 |
| Somewhere In Time, I Met You | 71 |
| Sometimes I Know | 75 |
| Steep Hills And Smooth Valleys | 76 |
| Surrender To Love Or Have Lust With-Out. | 77 |
| Surrender/Humility/Joy Equal: Action, Soul, And Heart. | 78 |
| Sweet Heart Of Mine, I Love You | 80 |
| The Law Of The Candle Light | 81 |
| The Mistress Of The Look | 82 |
| The Sight Of You Melts Me, You Are Chicken Soup For My Heart | 83 |
| The Wonderment Of It All | 84 |
| Valentine's Day And Crazy Love. | 86 |
| Walking By Faith | 87 |
| Walking In The Rain | 88 |
| What Do You Feel? | 90 |
| When I Think Of You | 93 |

| | |
|---|---|
| When Is My House A Home, Not Just On A Clear Day? | 94 |
| You May Be Away | 95 |
| Relax And Be Peaceful | 96 |
| Ain't It Wonderful; | 97 |
| The Color Of Rain? | 97 |
| A Place In My Dreams | 99 |
| Crazy Love And Beautiful Eyes | 101 |
| Grief And Love Loss | 102 |
| Grief And Love Come From The Same Heart And Loving Soul | 103 |
| Go For It, If You Dare | 104 |
| Last Time I Knew | 105 |
| Hurry, Time's Old… | 106 |
| Lonely One | 107 |
| I Will Be. I Am. | 108 |
| Snow Move Over. Shovels Are Here With Cheer-Wind Has Died Down | 109 |
| We Are | 110 |
| Time's Up, O''L Girl, You Wore Me Out And I'm Almost Dead. | 112 |
| Sweet Temptations, Married To Me | 113 |
| Spring Break | 114 |
| About the Author | 115 |

# A Love to Remember
## By RobertEatonSokol

A love to remember
Is full of light
From the sender.
It lets you surrender
To a kinder
Heart from the start,
Giving me a love to remember.

My soul is a sender, so
tender, Of," who I am," to
the world. I give it to you,
Lord, The fiber of my being.
Seeing your light adds
Radiant tenderness to my choices-
my world, and
Gives me a love to remember.

I made a decision
To give every day,
So, I can stay
In view of my blessings,
Of giving my love,
Un-tethered, to you,
What a love to remember.

Days vanish,
Touched by God.
Fill awe with your love,
Full of knowing,
Going through my life,
In your own loving way.
A love to remember.

# A Mother's Rain
## By RobertEatonSokol

The day grows young
And sweet as a mother's breast.
It rains, it slithers,
Drives and falls
From ridge to valley,
Flower to blade and
Seed to grain.
Petals stretch and reach,
Tips strain, bending
Toward the black and blue heavens.

I am wandering, as a drop of rain
Floating gently to the earth,
When all at once I see a rivulet
Of rain drops slide off a lone leaf
Into a dancing brook.
Suddenly, the air bursts with life,
And hundreds of flags of color
Hurl about, to and fro, in and out,
Gathering my little drops of rail
And hurling them back again.

# And so, It Goes to my Toes
## By RobertEatonSokol

You make me laugh.
You make me cry.
Please don't say good-by.

You make me smile.
You make me sigh.
Please don't tie me in knots.

You give me hope.
You give me miles of style.
Please don't be a dope of guile.

From the day we met,
We have set apart
The start of doves in flight
From the sight of joy and happiness.

From the moment I saw you,
My jaw set forward
Where it met your lips
And the tip of your tongue met mine.

When you opened my heart to laughter,
You lit a candle after
Warmth flowed from a load
Of love to my toes and so it goes.

## *Baby, It's Cold Outside, But Warm In Your Heart!*

By RobertEatonSokol

Upon your arrival,
I know there will be beams of
light At the sight of you,
But until then, I will wait
with Anticipation at the mere
Thought of your much sought-after delight.

Baby, it's cold outside,
But I am warmed,
Remembering the scents that lent
This memorable aroma
That lingers, singing
Swarthy notes that dote on my memory.

Let it snow, send a glow
Marked by a thaw
In the chill so your bill
Will loosen my stiff gills.
Let me in. don't flaunt the din.
You know, I wait in spite of this chill.

Baby, its cold, but you are hot.
I've just got to see you and
When I do....
Well, blue I won't be while waiting to see
Your sparkling smile.
Please let me in?

# *Between You And Me*
## By RobertEatonSokol

Waves lap at wharf piling
Wearing there, just a bit…
They were born at the ripple
Of a pebble of rain
They slide softly over floating drift wood;
Tumble over hollowed caverns of air left
Vacant by the last one,
Bubble over clods of sea weed
Left carelessly by natures' furrow,
Where time has burrowed.

Sea weed is left to dry
And star fish die
As we lie in my soft, dry bed
Shaking from its spite and light
Flashing in the night.

A mist forms
The winds beneath are still.
Fins glide along, brushing
The billowing sand,
Cutting at boulders in a gracious attempt
At molding them; moving them sensuously, in and out.
Gills beating in a silky rhythm,
And amoeba fills cracks and corners
While coral paint the salty mixture
By merely existing,
Giving the canvas a delicate, moving texture.

Down there, the eye takes
In a curious reality.
It is violent but the fish
Calmly swim; it is calm
And the sea weed merely sway
In an attempt to provide
A screen of invisibility.

## *Black Is Cool and Powered by Joy*
### By RobertEatonSokol

Black is a color to remember
As I am a sender of my history.
Even as my skin appears white,
I miss my black grandmother's warm brown
Smile and loving pat on my head; "Good night."

So, I am so very sad when I see
The dictionary's view of color where
Black is equated with sad and bad
While white is synonymous with pure white angels.
What I know is: Human kind was born black and
beautiful, And White light can be blinding,
So, I am not confused or even amused.

The cool of the night massages
My eyes from the bright of the day passed,
As I closed my eyes to bay
At beckoning sleep.
Blackness gives comfort to find my dreams.

Black is the color of the void
From which my life is built.
The power of this color
Gives amazing respect to
The milieu of the morning dew.

Just imagine the awesome views of God's splendor
When Black is the view of so much of who we are.
Joy is in the Senses as we appreciate
All the smells, tastes and eye candy
Of much of what we are about, The
rainbow, fruited flavors and
The tantalizing sizzles that greet us at
home, Beckoning our noses.

I feel the pride of hearts
Blended by colors of brothers and sisters
Trying to find a place in this space
Where my color does not appear
As important as my Creator's word,
The color of rain.

Of this I am certain, I can imagine
How bored I would be without
The zing of character building
Of the luscious skin tones,
Delicious black lips Smiling me to sleep,
Where diamonds keep.

Black is so much more than a color.
The mere mention of blackness gives bold clarity
To the nature of our universe where
Invisibility is trumped by the power
Of our very nature, where we are born,
Not torn asunder.

Black is a back to back aligning of the purity of our Creator's
Wishes and the root of our real view of you and me.

# Curious Mind and Ruby Red Lips
By RobertEatonSokol

Ruby red lips peak
My curious mind, where
They find
Delicious thoughts of wonder,
Claps of thunderous excitement,
Filled with sensuous dreams.

Full pouty lips
Trip me with delight,
Winks and nods, directing kindness,
Curing blindness with their brightness.
Curious, enquiring mind, signed on for,
Probing, strobing, prancing and dancing,
Giving delight to her measured message.

Sensuous full ruby red lips,
Leave a curious glow,
Flowing from a tone,
Sewn from wondrous softness,
And grown from a seemingly endless heart.
They leave an audience of one,
Breathless from the encounter.

Does this mean she will visit again?

## *Discover the Beginning*

```
   LOVE
    AT
   THE
BOTTOM
    OF
    A
   KISS   WHERE
            SMILE
             IS
            THE
            TOP
             OF
             A
           WINK AND
                 WRINKLE
                    IS
                   THE
                   DIRT
                   FROM
                   THE
                   FROWN.
```

By RobertEatonsokol

## *Fire Flies, Twinkling Stars and Goose Bumps*
By RobertEatonSokol

When you look at me
You touch my faith;
It becomes greater
And every day grows deeper.
When you touch my hand,
You ignite my imagination,
Making it expand beyond
All reason, leaving
Sparks of wonder throughout my soul.
When you touch my ear,
I hear the power of my spirit
Ringing with excitement
From the moment of "yes,"
Giving new zeal to the elimination
Of all my fears so I can hear you
whisper, "I love you."

When you touch my back,
The tingling strength of character
Erupts with a power reserved
For giants, but since I am not one,
I will bask in your touch
Alone, giving me memories
Of fire flies and rockets exploding.
When you wash my feet,
You opened the tap
Of my humble love
And it flows with understanding

Giving order to power and harmony,
The glue in my heart,
From the start.
This is our life,
Our gift from God
To stand under; with wonderful
Baskets of roses
And bushels of fruit from the
bowels Of glory in spirit.
So, God blesses us with
Hours of shimmering fireflies
and Twinkling stars.

## *Fishing for Goodness*
By RobertEatonSokol

A cup of spiced tea in November,
Left my taste buds with something to remember.
Sure, it was cold out,
But it was not about
The bate, but this stately catch.

Ah, the fish were biting,
And the lures were sighting
All the best game.
But that wasn't the same
As seeing your reflection.

Releasing my lured rod,
I beckoned with crooked finger
And a smile that lingers
To this day, as if to say
"You are welcome in this stream's beam."

But no, you prefer, To
secure the shore Where lore
is sewn and Tease comes
with a breeze As you
winked and I blinked

So, my rod has found a nod,
And the reel winds in a flurry,
To retrieve, not leave, this catch.
The fish may fight at this sight,
But your sight is my trophy.

## *Found Love*

By RobertEatonSokol

We find love
When feeding a lost dog,
When loving a scared cat,
Finding a piece of driftwood;
Wait a bit,
Then climbing a cliff to know it better;
Watch a sunset from a silo top,
Slide down a hill of leaves
To be caught in each other's arms
At the bottom where a soft kiss is planted.
Not a second is wasted
Nor a thought or minute sacrificed,
But all given with the thought of love.
I care.

# Gift

## By RobertEatonSokol

I just saw the most beautiful sight.
A squirrel sitting on top of a telephone pole, eating a nut...
A mother bird feeding her young...
The sun folding up for the day…
A rabbit kissing another...
A worm surfing the dirt…
A tiny kitten suckling its mother...
the sun on a pebble of dew on a lily pad...
A happy smile after a frown...
A cat and dog eating together…
A warm heart…
Mom and dad kissing with love…
A gift, love.

## *How Do I Know*
### By RobertEatonSokol

In the softness of the moon light
I walk to the water's edge
Just to wait for you.

In the dew of the stars' night
I am drawn towards you
Moon glow so I cannot go,
But the wink knows.

In the twinkle of the sun's breath,
I walk towards this dusty road
Just to catch a glimpse of your
image, Just so I can breathe.

In this noon day brightness
I am within your spirit
Where I am meant to be,
So, I can be complete.

So how do I know?
I know by the sight
Of your shimmering face;
By the laughter sounds,
Knowing no bounds;

I know by the touch of your tickling
finger, Not lingering for taste;
Because my funny bone tingles
When you jingle my chain;
I know because my mind is so sure,
It cannot stop to wonder if;
Just because I know.

I know because my soul is at peace
Within my heart.
I know I love you
Because I do not have to ask why.

## *Gratitude and Thankfullness*

By RobertEatonSokol

When I give my love,
I really do not expect to receive gratitude.
But it comes anyway;
There is no latitude and my heart know.

When I show empathy,
I really do not expect appreciation.
But it comes anyway, without depreciation.
It is an understanding without branding.

When I express thankfulness,
I do not expect acknowledgement.
But it comes whether I want it or not.
It is a knowing, a suggestive look.

When I see your eyes,
I am never surprised,
Just delighted at the
Power gratitude has over ego.

As I see joy give power
To vulnerability, it is never sour.
It is only a reflection of Love and empathy
And I appreciate the respect I earn.

No surprise, just thankful for gratitude.
It is an unlicensed peace that replaces
Ego with the power of love.

## *Happy Dance*
By RobertEatonSokol

Oh, my mind is filled
With expectations, spilling
Over with delight in spite of
My lack of a view, of you.

Ah, as my mind's eye fills the sky
With glee, gee whiz and by golly,
I am filled with smiles for a while,
Never letting go of my memory of your

prance. Wow, says the glint of glee, as

Your dancing head sways to and
fro, Sopping up the sight of me,
Hopping back and forth for the touch we must have.

As I fairly fly towards your memory,
I glance to the sky and say,
"My, my, my, your love is what I drive

for." As I get closer,

I actually slow my go-to-her,
So, I can bask in the sight
Of your delight and smile, punctuated
by "Hurry, hurry, don't slow now."

I find the steps I take are stepped and
measured So, I can soak up your glee with me.
"Just a few moments longer," say I.

And as I near the top
I am overcome with your warm smile,
Holding me for miles before dialing your number.

The memory of your prancing dance
Makes my lips curl and my eyes list with mist,
Lest I take too much time of mine to reach your lips.

Love is a happy dance.

## *Real Joy, Strength and Courage Is Born from Love*

RobertEatonSokol

HIM:
Snuggling under my blanket
With my head nestled in the pillow of your tummy,
Is the comfort that gives me strength.
Feed me this warmth and my heart
Will be yours for the life of this poem, it never ends.

Closing my eyes is the cocoon
That feeds my tummy;
The food for tender dreams.
Folding my arms around you
And simply holding you
As we shimmer in our caresses,
Is the power from which courage is born.

When I say I love you,
I will do anything for you.

HER:
After first glances and lust's wondrous entangled
dance, Captivated by love and Momentary passions
spent, After the seduction of the unknown is known
and Fevers calm—the fire burns brightly and strong.
After the loving, the real loving begins---

With the touch, sight and embraces that excite the senses.
The gentle reminders of caring, "how can I help you,"
The smells of "pieaou" coming from the kitchen,
The daily expressions of love that engage every part of
Our spirits. The way your smile lights up the room when I enter.
The delight you show when being of service to me and others.
In good and challenging times your
Love is unwavering even if I may appear to fluctuate.

No plans for imprisoning the passions of intertwined spirits,
They flow as they must, even as we know---
After the loving, the real loving begins.

# *How Do I Know?*

In the softness of the moon light
I walk to the water's edge
Just to wait for you.

In the dew of the stars' night
I am drawn towards your
Moon glow so I cannot go, but the wink knows.

In the twinkle of the sun's breath,
I walk towards this dusty road
To catch a glimpse of your image, just so I can breathe.

In this noon day brightness
I am within your spirit
Where I am meant to be, so I can be complete.

So how do I know?
I know by the sight
Of your shimmering face;
By the sounds of laughter,
Knowing no bounds.

I know by the tough of your tickling
finger, Not lingering for taste,
Because my funny bone tingles
when You jingle my chain.

I know because my mind is so sure,
It cannot stop to wonder if;
Just because I know.
I know because my mind is at peace
Within my heart.

I know I love you because I do not have to ask why.

    RobertEatonSokol

## *How Do I Love You &*
## *Butterfly Kisses?*
By RobertEatonSokol

Let me show you,
See my glow;
It lets you know that I served
Those seeds of" please don't go."

Let me know; touch me with your
glance; Let's slow dance
And I will whisper, in a trance,
"I love you," softly." I love you."

Let me send dwelling smells to your delight.
Let me share my passion for
Aromas, the art of roads to your heart,
Wafting to your nose, swelling our sizzle.

How do I love you?
The many ways I lay in
Your look-of-butter-fly-kisses,
Lily-pad winks, blinks and nods.

## How Long Are Your Fingers? Let's Have Diner.

By RobertEatonSokol

If they can play the piano,
They can sooth my hair,
Peeling away layers of players.

If they can play the violin,
They can smooth any fear,
Nurturing my heart and soul

If they can pluck my guitar,
They can reassure my arm
And make me feel safe.

As we sit to eat, this gourmet seat
Allows our view of each other,
Giving another view of
The music that serenades our hearts.
From your fingers to my heart,
What a sizzle!

## *How Will I Find You?*
### By RobertEatonSokol

How could I miss,
My kiss on your lips?
You left your mark!

Will I see your smile, visible for
miles? It's bound in my memory and
I am not blind!

Maybe it would be your eyes.
They light my sky! I could not
Avoid the rainbow!

Could it be your walk?
Since your gate talks,
I cannot miss you!

If I hear your entry,
Down the gentry, it happens
With words not heard.

Your very presence
Carries the essence of
Birds singing!

Laugh kookaburra, laugh
In this old
Gum tree.

You make me smile all the while.
It must be you
I'm looking for.

## *I Am High On Feeling*

By RobertEatonSokol

Every day is the first day;
It is filled with the
Joy of just being here.
The tingle in my fingers
Is the freedom of my choosing?

I am high on joy
Every morning I open my eyes
To the sun's light
Where I see good
Rise above all evil.

I am high on wonderment
At the beginning of each day,
For the love of my God's heart
Because I am one
With you and your soul.

I am clear in your vision
As I see your light
Through my mind's eye
Where my high is
The effervescence of all life.

It is your endowment of meaning and joy
That enriches my heart and soul.
It is the power you give me
That lifts me from the
Heated bowels of earth
So, I can luxuriate in your light.

I am high on the bubbles of
joy That I felt from the
Memory of meeting You the
first time,
And then I met me.
Thank you for the introduction

## *I am an Idea in the Mind of God and I am Here.*

By RobertEatonSokol

I woke up in the morning
To the light of your smile.
It gives me power to keep my heart beating.
The simple mindfulness of
God's word is my power
To share with you.

I woke up this morning
To the sea of god.
What can you see?
Not much of me.
It's below the surface there
The sun doesn't shine,
So, you have to look a little
To find where I am.

I woke up this morning
Ready to surrender
To the excitement
In my heart
Meant for you, my loving friend.

## *I Am The Lucky One,*
## *But It Is Not Luck At All*
By RobertEatonSokol

Grace came to me.
I found it because
It fits God's view of you.
I could not resist as
Joy lifted my eyes.

As I put aside resistance in favor of
the Flavor of awareness,
Bowls full of soulful healing began.
Joy and resistance could not together be so,
 I asked and prayed for balance from Thee.
And out of the blue I
found you.

"I wish I could, I hope I can," created clouds
Of confusion. Just as surely as fear ruled and
Its' comfort lulled me, joy culled me from the crowd.
I found acceptance and knowing, is an acknowledgement
Of my dealing in feelings in unexpected ways.
I was lost, and I found my way, today.
You make me feel brand new.

Yonder distance did not "make" my heart
grow Fonder. Miles between us allowed me
To see your grace more clearly,
As the fog cleared. It is you I see.
As I see my mirror, there is no longer confusion.
The delusions of the past find nothing
To hold on to.

The genie in the sky is your grace in this
place Called love. As I think of you,
I say "You betcha, by golly and wow."
You are the one who I've been waiting for;
My love for you grows higher and higher,
I sigh, as I spy grace.
It's you, too.

# *I Thought about You!*
## By RobertEatonSokol

I love what you said!
Say it again!
I love your eyes.
They are soft, yet powerful.

I love what you said!
Say it again!
I like your strong nose.
It detects the best of aromas.

I love what you said!
Say it again!
I like your ears.
They know the music of love.

I love what you said!
Say it again!
I love your mouth.
It sings your song and knows my kiss.

I love what you said!
Say it again, please!
I crave your touch.
It gives me power for today and the morrow.
I love you, I said it again.

## *If Only I Could Be Forever*
By RobertEatonSokol

If only I had met you,
When I was younger,
I would not have hungered
For happiness so much of
My years, full of fear and regret.
It was a test of character building.

If only I did not have those flaws
I held within my soul;
I would have shared more of this bowl
Of good tidings that were with-in reach.
I could share them or rid them.

If only I could out-live me,
I would give to thee, my love,
My mended and whole soul,
That was infected at birth.
I would give you unfettered love,
Given to me from above for thee.

If only you can wait,
Until I am whole,
You will find a bold soul,
Full of hope, kindness and gratitude;
Given from birth but hidden by blindness,
Not wanting to grow up, for you.

If you can keep your mind when
Those about you are not, then,
I can only bless and trust me and Thee.
Please do not tire of waiting. I gave it to
thee. I will not be here forever,
But my heart and soul are and ever yours.

If I could only be forever, I would make my dreams,
Ours for hours. It is upon this imperfect landscape
That I proclaim my undying love to you.
Where else could I look
Except through your eyes,
And into your soul where you await mine.
I love you.

## *Inspiration:*
### By RobertEatonSokol

I know the truth.
It clears the muddy water.

I am one with truth.
It gives me power to love.

I am at peace
Within my soul, where God leads me.

I feel invincible
In my heart, where I am whole.

# *The Beginning, The Middle, The End*

| THE BEGINNING | THE MIDDLE | THE END |
|---|---|---|
| Love at The Bottom of A Kiss | Smile Is the Top of A Wink | Wrinkle Is the Dirt from The Frown |

By RobertEatonSokol        2004

## *It Was In November When We Met.*
### By RobertEatonSokol

It was November,
The autumn of my year,
When we really met. We set
In motion a commotion
The likes of which we had not
Been subjected to before.
Please, I want more.

Star dust found dandelion seeds
Floating, looking for safe landings;
The winds of time caught them as they
Waited for a lift to prosperity.
After much sought after thought,
They sprinkled my face,
Much to the delight of your curled lips.

I found you in October, giving me something
To remember in November.
Close your eyes
And dance within this love,
Sway to the beat,
Heating this seat in my heart.
Does it get any better?

So then came December,
And you popped your head out.
Just ask your mother. She
Surrendered to the excitement
That was meant
For me and thee to see.

## *Its Not Always As It Seems, Or Is It?*

By RobertEatonSokol

Is this a mirage
Or is my mind
Playing tricks
When I think I see your face?

When will we see the message as truth?
Will you have to think?
Or am I a messenger of wonder and tease
Wishing to please your taste buds?

With all the choices,
When will you know?
It is really the right time
To believe in your heart.

Was it the wink?
Or the smirk that got you?
Was it the soft word?
Or the gentile touch what sent the spark?

One thing I know is, I love you.
You got me, yesterday,
Today and tomorrow.
My heart knows, I hope you do too.

I think it was my struggle,
Though it seemed effortless,
For which something greater was born
To you.

## *Pink is my Favorite Color*
### By RobertEatonSokol

Please smile when you look
Inside my body; it's PINK!
You cannot look at this color without
Knowing its Heavenly source.

Every mother knows that
Behind every smile,
Inside every wink, and
On every tongue is the color, PINK.

If you think you can blink,
Without a snicker of delight,
'tis a smile that will swell into gee whiz.
Drink up, it is PINK!

Women embrace it!
Men sigh when she walks by.
There is no disgrace in embracing this child.
The smile knows.
IT'S PINK, YOU KNOW.

## Just A Little Bit, Can Make Me Do Great Things

By RobertEatonSokol

All I want
Is a steady hand and your touch.
It softens the land.

All I really need
Is your kind word and herds of kisses.
They make me want to "be a better man."

All I lead with
Is my power, molded by your smile
It melts away all my fear.

All the speed
I charge with is fueled
By your encouraging love.

All the imagination
I can muster is inspired
Merely by your twinkling eyes.

Men are just puppy dogs.
Treat them with a wink
And all they need is a good mistress
To wag their tails...

# Kings And Queens: Would-Be
## By RobertEatonSokol

If you think you are the king of your house,
But have not yet met the queen-to-be-spouse,
You might be an illusion in her lair.
The delusion, you experience, is a man's ego
Tugging at your stupid light.

Men would be king
If they know where the queen be.
Women can make the crown and
All they need is an invitation,
Of adoration and respect, detecting real love.

Men will find their real power,
When they honor their would-be queen,
Otherwise seen as confusing their moments.
Men's need to be important is captured
By their Queens need for safety, where their heart swells.

Amazingly, when a man acknowledges the
heart Of the woman they find their heart
And crown awaiting them. It is as simple as
Adoring her and her place in your space. The
lace She adds becomes the fabric for your life.

The path to your new crown and kingdom is as easy to find
as Allowing and owning vulnerability, empathy and
Intimacy. The keys to her heart and mind
Are adorned by truth and the invitation
For her to come in from the cold.

## Let's Dance!
### By RobertEatonSokol

Let's dance
In this stance of love!

Please take my hand, let it
land In place of wasted grace.

Bless fear. Let's melt,
The confusion we felt.

Let me gaze into your eyes,
So, they can lead us in sighing delight.

Grab this moment.
Let it lead us past lust,
And into surrender of bodies,
Allowing sashaying and swaying.
Sense the beholding aroma,
Of getting sweat.

Humming the tune of the loon,
Might advance us to June,
Where we discover
The mother of invention; lovers
Molding soft spirits,
Dancing the night away.

# *Life Statement:*
## *It Is All Good And It Is God.*
By RobertEeatonSokol

I woke up this morning
Making room for passion
In my heart.
It gives me power
To share with you.

I woke up this morning
Feeling my passion
For life in my mind.
The fire in my soul's belly
Fills my spirit with
Fuel reserved for life alone.

I had lunch today
On the food of opportunity
For good to be shared
With all of you.
The spirit lives for eternity.

I am having dinner with you
Now and forever so I can
Feed on the wealth of God's
Table of love. It feeds me
And the music fills my heart.
Let's dance.

## *I Am An Idea In The Mind Of God And I Am There.*

I woke up this morning
To the light of your smile
It gives power to keep my heart beating.
The simple mindfulness of
God's word is my power
To share with you.

I woke up this morning
To the sea of God
What can you see?
Not much of me.
It's below the surface where
The sun doesn't shine,
So, you have to look a little
To find where I am.

I woke up this morning
Ready to surrender
To the excitement in my heart
Meant for you, my loving friend.

## Listen
### By RobertEatonSokol

Listen and you will hear
As the wind leaves
Rustling leaves to
Quiet the day.

Listen and you will hear Soft
breezes melt Snow, belting out
Gurgling notes, gloating About
its power, lending it's Dowry to
morning glory's Trumpeting
their delight Through morn to
dusk light until

They musket Hello at morn before
sewing Our noses with their glory.

Listen and you will hear
Soft rain slithering down ice daggers,
Checking the weakness in my heart,
Turning it to bold strokes where I am
Told hello from below,
As if that is all there is.
But no, there are the crocus
And jonquil playing peak-a-boo
With the glow of our visions delight.

Listen and you will hear
Warming ice cracking its way
To nurturing the slow hand below.

Let it touch you
And gently go
Where none should. Blow with
Warm breath and melt the snow.
Serve me a cup of orange spice tea
And vanish the chill. And with your breath,
Warm my ears. Then wrap your arms
Around this blanket of character
And call it love.

# *My Addiction Is Love and Significance*
By RobertEatonSokol

What I noticed was
How warm I felt
When you leaned
Your back against my chest
So, I could encircle you
With my arms, radiating our warmth,
Touch to touch.

What I noticed when you turned
Toward me,
Was the warmth
That ascended from
Your eyes to mine.
It is your gaze of caring
Daring me to be greater than I am.

What I felt
Was how strong
I stood, humble and not mumbling
This song.
I belong to this moment
As long as I am alive,
I can survive.

"You are my sunshine,
My only sunshine.
You make me happy,
When I am grey.
You'll never know dear,
How much I love you.
Please don't take
My sunshine away."

# *My Best Friend, My Love, How I See Thee*

By RobertEatonSokol

I do know how I feel,
The soft/glad passion
When we laugh together;
Our hearts glow.

I know the strength I feel
When we share secrets,
Those intimate feelings
And deep concerns.

I know the feeling I have
When you touch me
Softly, knowingly;
You take my breath away.
You give me power to be.

I know how high I am,
Knowing you are there.
I know how strong and secure I feel
When you have my heart key.
It is the trust, the never-ending love.

I know how I see you,
Forever steering us through life's confusing moments.
We walk so proudly,
Through our live together.
My spirit is strong,
The memory of your breath,
Against my cheek.
You are my smile, every day of my life.
Thee, I love. This I do know.

# *My Goddess, She Lives With-In Me.*

By RobertEatonSokol

**J**     Just when I thought peace was here **U**
Up rose a clatter. It did not matter that **A** All
you give is given unto me.
**N**Now that you have entered my soul,
**I** It occurs to me that the clarity of this moment **T** Takes
its place in my heart, where you are taking **A** Action in
healing souls. You are the definition of
       Goodness.

**L**     Love is the gift you give me and the breath I breathe.
**I**      It comes from your heart, a leaf on God's tree where
the **V** Very blood that feeds the tree is the
**E**Everlasting food for my
**S**Soul, the strength of my belly's fire.

**I**     If there is humility in finding perfection, then
**N** Never expecting failure is not an option.

**M**    Maybe, finding happiness is as simple as
**E**Entering this place and calling it Juanita.

## *It's My Heart, Not A Burp Left From Your Hurt*

By RobertEatonSokol

The safety of spirit, freely shared and not spared,
Can be compromised instantly when
My fear clouds my spirit
And then my heart. The tether That
holds us together comes from A deeper
place where my soul's Foundation
stitches our hearts together. This is
where the power of willingness Creates
the magic of forgiveness.

I take responsibility and then forgive myself for
What I don't know, don't understand or
Even see. The answer is to listen, then
Release fear when I say, "I love you;"
I cut any tether to you. Fly away just for a day.
Do not spare me, butterfly, fly if you must
But don't lust after the windy dust.
The trust you find may be fleeting,
Without any soft greeting. It is, after all,
Dusty must. I will be here,
When you be. Be still and see
This is where my heart is. It's me.

## My Ride With Destiny
### By RobertEatonSokol

On my ride with destiny,
I felt smiles by miles
Greet me from the
Wow, with warmth
To bait my beating heart with.

I could feel you
Stealing a glance
Just to see if
I noticed the twinkle
In your eyes.

It is not a question
Of if I know,
Just that I am booked,
Hooked on you.
Give me a break…And you did.

Your stake in this session
Is a lesson in mindful contact
So, the impact is filled
With splendid explosions
Lending tinkling sensations to the air.

I love you.
That is my Destiny.
It was just waiting
To be heard so my
Word had been spoken,
Not as a token.
My heart is yours, alone.

## *New Choices Today*
By RobertEatonSokol

I wish you were here
To caress my sore hands.
They till and toil in earth
To feed our souls spanning the universe.

I wish you were here
To soothe my back.
Tired from carrying the weight of
My life joys and misery sacks.

I wish you were here
To encourage my bruised legs;
Tired from many trudging dusty miles
Of effort, begging to rest.

I wish you were here
To wash my tired feet,
Dusty from this journey of heart
Please honor this seat, reserved for you and God.

I know you are going to stay.
To play after our victory
Over sadness and lacking,
Left from our stray wars.
You are welcome.
Please stay and play.

# Not Just Any Goddess
## By RobertEatonSokol

| | |
|---|---|
| **J** | Just as I open my eyes |
| **U** | Up you stand, demanding |
| **A** | Attention by stature alone. |
| **N** | Never not intriguing, |
| **I** | It occurs to others |
| **T** | That you are worth |
| **A** | Attitude with gratitude. |
| | |
| **G** | Give me a moment |
| **O** | Of atonement so I can regain |
| **D** | Dignity lost to spared errors. |
| **D** | Direct my spirit so |
| **E** | Every waking moment is |
| **S** | Spent knowing your |
| **S** | Spirit, in its grandeur. |
| | |
| **O** | Oh, give my heart a home. |
| **F** | Forget that I am just a man and let me see All of your breast formed heart. |
| | |
| **M** | Make your treasure my field of dreams, |
| **I** | Incarnated in my eyes, where |
| **N** | Neigh is only for weaker souls |
| **E** | Ever pressing for greater |

heights. God bless you and me.

## *Our Love Is Here To Stay*
By RobertEatonSokol

Our love never dies.
It is there when,
We awake from a nap. It is,
At the end of a sip of cold air,
Or at the foot of an airport walkway.

Our love is heard,
In the morning,
And the evening,
Even in grieving.

Our love is here
To stay,
So, we can play,
At what may come today.

Some say they are amazed,
But it was love at first sight.
I was and still am, it is not a plan,
Totally immersed in my love for you.

Our love is felt,
When our eyes meet at the street,
Where our chest beat is heard as words,
Of courage, lifting us to sight and light.
Our love is here to stay.

## Partnership: A Process
By RobertEatonSokol

We met, seeking to set
In motion, a notion
Of emotional commotion.
A gust of love dust blew in.

You felt my gaze rise,
Like a warm blanket,
Building a wondrous cocoon.
So soon, you might wonder?

Can we relate, not debate?
From the gate? So, we send
Invitations to share tokens
Of spoken, unbroken promises.

We keep looking for links,
Not kinks so we can
Explore, not ignore, the possibilities.
There are plans that span
The time of mine and yours so it
Becomes ours for future hours.

There-it becomes trust,
A must, for friendship so we
Can create a partnership where
Love becomes the building
Blocks from above.

Not wanting to
Remain separate, we
determined That friendship was
not enough. So, we love and
add sprinkles of Blinks, winks,
and nod Build miles of smiles,
Warm hearts, and even brain farts.

Partners are we,
As auras fly over and around us
With glints, even hints of grandeur,
Sounding billows of gladness
Instead of sadness. What we
Find is a partnership to celebrate.

## *Pieaou: A Special Flavoring Born Of Love.*

By RobertEatonSokol/JLC

At first whiff, you sigh,
The pie has such character,
And the folks say,
"It is to die for, even lie for."
So, quick, buy it from the guy
In the kitchen. But he will say,
No, only love cooks here, and
Love is not for sale."

Frustrated at being turned away
From such pieaou, my taste buds,
No duds, said ouch, as I slouched in
My couch. This pieaou carries a flavor.
That urges savor.
So, I gave her my flavor
To remember my salute.

Pieaou is the glue,
For all new stew, saluting
The vegetables I slew.
It is the mood for food,
The result from a glint of love.
The thought, alone, flavors the aroma.

Please Invite Every mother,
Aunt and grandmother to share
The aroma over us.

## *Please Wait For Me, I Will Be There Soon.*

By RobertEatonSokol

Let me not hold my tears!
They will fill me
With the noise of joy!

Let me see your face,
Don't hide it with lace,
So, I can race to your grace!

Allow my love to fly
With doves so I can let go of the fears
That held my tears for years.

Happy are my feet,
Moving briskly in the street.
I will boldly hold you soon.

Let me by these others
Who smother their midst…?
It is God's heart speaking and leaking.

I am so glad not to be sad!
The mere thought of you
Is the daring view, so?

Please wait for me,
I am moving briskly
Deliberately, toward our meeting.

As I spied you,
The sky opened, not a cloud seen,
There is sheen over my cheeks as we do Hello.

## *Poetry In Motion*
### By RobertEatonSokol

It is in your mouth as you part your
lips; They broaden to a smile.
Your tongue touches your teeth, As
men shutter in weak-kneed awe.

It is in your eyes.
They have a smile of their own.
Their laser power pierce men's armor.
And makes weak puppies.

Men are instantly mesmerized,
Captivated As you sashay in any
direction; And the uncanny part is
After they are completely flustered,
You talk, and they are blown away.

Men are your puppies,
They live for a cuddle.
Pet them and their wagging tail
Follows them as they strut with such pride.
Scratch their ears and
They perk up for more
Their eyes soften like warm chocolate
As she praises, they're adorable
Smile—what suckers?

## *Self Worth And Value*
"I know the man. I know the truth."

By RobertEatonSokol

How happy I would be if….
If I could see what's hidden
In the fields filed with
Daisy's smiling their way to
Peak-a-boo in a sea of wafting wheat.
There is no sound except for
The touches of grass blades
As they salute God's wonder.
The focus is on your spirit,
Where we find all inspiration.

The joy we feel is not in bondage of past memories,
But in the healing of all spirit.
The past does not apply,
Otherwise it rules the future.
What is mine to own or not,
Is the memory, alone.
What moves me is this moment
And it is mine to keep or let go of.
I, alone, am responsible for its wealth.

When you release yourself,
You discover a love,
You never before thought possible.
And the power I receive,
Makes my heart invincible

Love is my freedom and
All I need to do is to claim it.
These are only words but
They give clarity to all my passion.
It is joy, peace and love that builds my heart.
This is truth in its own power.
The rest is in the affirmation.

# *She Walked In*
## By RobertEatonSokol

Beautiful brown eyes
Soften the pain of snapped necks
No argument, here.
Effervescent, pearly smile,
Quicken happy thoughts;
She turns gazes down
The folds of her gown.
Add men to her sound.

Soft brown eyes,
Are the stuff of need
Filled with seeds
Of hope, desire and passion—
The I's say, wow!
But how does she feel?
She's full of zeal, the real deal.
With the dirt of neglect
I detect the deeds
So, what are your needs?

What leads to the soft Folds of
warm touches? Thoughtful hands
assure, It's OK? What is more?
Where is the bite?
I then ask myself, "Why do our needs seem so
similar;" And then restrain my heart'
Though my mind and soul raise for her Praise.

## So Much In Love, It's More Than Titles For Right Living
RobertEatonSokol

Oh girl, I'd be in trouble,
If you left me now.
You are my lady.
It could be my dream.
We were only making love and
You are my gravy daisy.

I see your face in every way,
Even in the morning,
Like the early dew.
I see your face everywhere,
Even in the evening
Swaying to the music.

All I need is the music in your eyes,
It's in the magic of your sighs.
As we prance, dancing into the night.
You are once, twice, three times my lady.
You are my soul molding, holding
My spring and summer, our season for joy.

God bless you,
You make me feel brand new.
Good times, bad times, I feel renewed.
Whenever you want me, I'll be there.
Whenever you see me,
I'll be your soul man, with a bowl of wishes.

# Soft Rain Or Delicate Snow
### By RobertEatonSokol.

The sound of soft rain,
Defines the delicate
Feeling I share
When I say," I love you."

The nurturing we give
Through touching our hearts,
Clarifies how cleansed and
Fresh we feel when we say, "me too."

Can you hear the snow?
It quiets the soft rain,
As it lightly passes my eyes
On its silent way to touching my heart.

Can you feel?
The delicate aroma,
Surrounding each snow flake,
Cleansed by God's breath?

Do you know the wonder?
Of truth in each drop of rain,
Of each unique flake of snow
That defines my heart and my God?

Follow the warm or cold moisture
And be amazed by each one,
Before it settles on the once,
Dry dark earth stones and blades of grass.

There you will find
A rainbow of splendor.

Just imagine the joy
Of receiving God's loving wonder,
Drop after drop, flake after flake,
Imagine the child's joy
When God shines his eyes
On this moistened ground, so they can play again.

Feel the excitement as
They shout their glee
At the renewed thought
Of freedom.

## *Somewhere In Time, I Met You*
### By RobertEatonSokol

Somewhere in time
There is a love
Which knows no one but me,
Though it seems to be without.

 Somewhere in time
I met you,
And the senses were so powerful
That it seemed that they came out of a fog
Into a blaze of delight.

Somewhere in time
I saw you and
I knew it was the last
Of the emotions I would ever want.
It was so immense, and the intent was;

In my time
I held your hand and
My heart leapt from my chest
To yours, only
I could not get close enough
To touch you or clutch you.

Somewhere in time
I closed my eyes
And dreamed of your face,
Your hands, your breasts against mine.
We were so incredibly close.

It will be a memory
All of its own. I loved you so.

Just as suddenly as
You came into my vision,
My red tears flowed over and over my dried face.
Fleeting is the sight of your flowing lace,
If I can see you only in my dreams,
I will close my eyes as often
As the cream melts in my coffee.
I will hold them closed as long as I can and Open them to
your eyes
Only when they are there.

If I must, I will trust my heart
That you will be there.
I will wait for only your voice
And revel in its sound.
Thinking of the love we share.

I will do whatever I must to Retrieve
it, follow it, work it, Move boulders,
but faithfully Remove you from
whatever danger Might Fall in front of
your gliding feet, Where ever they
are.

The music I hear from your song
Lifted me, and brought me a heart
So bright and bold,
So soft and tender, it had no equal.

So, I will wait somewhere in time,
For a love which I have only dreamed of.
This is a memory meant for kings, and lovers.

So, as I sleep,
The dreams I have will have to
Keep my heart gentle and strong.
From this day forward and on.

I will have this goal in time.
It will be to single mindedly win
You this time for our place in time.
Ah, yes, the mountain may be tall,
The hills steep, but none of that
Will keep me from fulfilling what
Is our place in our space. Where else
Will we find such parallel peace and joy?

    All of its own. I loved you so.

Just as suddenly as
You came into my vision,
My red tears
Flowed over and over my dried face.
Fleeting is the sight of your flowing lace,
If I can see you only in my dreams,
I will close my eyes as often
As the cream melts in my coffee.
I will hold them closed as long as I can
and Open them to your eyes Only when
they are there.

If I must, I will trust my
heart That you will be there.
I will wait for only your voice
And revel in its sound. Thinking of the love we
share. I will do whatever I must to
Retrieve it, follow it, work it,

Move boulders, but faithfully

Remove you from whatever danger might
Fall in front of your gliding feet,
Where ever they are. The music
I hear from your song
Lifted me, and brought me a heart
So bright and bold,
So soft and tender, it had no equal.

## *Sometimes I Know*
### By RobertEatonSokol

Sometimes I know how
To show what I feel
Or how I radiate my love,
While you dine on my heart.

Sometimes I know how
Good you are, now
That I see you're shining
Smile, while I look for you.

Sometimes I know you,
When you touch me; I smile
At our love for the clear
Dignity in my peace.

I know why,
"Easy," is not in my dreams
Of the goodness in our hearts.
It is so grand.
We raise our gaze to the moon's glow.

There is no doubt,
Of the softness
In the rays of tenderness
Waiting for you,
Every time we share our eyes.

## Steep Hills And Smooth Valleys
By RobertEatonSokol

Come sleep with me.
Make love to my heart.
Drink coffee with me;
Add cream and sugar to start then,
Sip the warmth again and again and
Let your tongue savor the ascending flavor.

Come wake with me
After my toes curl from the joy of your part.
When the cup empties from your lips,
All that is left is a drip from the start
Of sugar, cream and coffee and
The aroma from your smile.

Come fly with me
When your silky cape ruffles in
The early morning breeze,
The twinkle in your eyes
Will light up the AM sky.
Come fly away with me, come fly away.

## *Surrender To Love Or Have Lust With-Out.*

By RobertEatonSokol

If you feel you must
Lust, you spurn trust and
Find pleasure with intention.
Peace and intimacy do not live where
Truth is a mixed bag, it lags.
Surrender to love. Let its power tower,
And leave behind the illusions of ego. Open
Your eyes with no lies and you may find
Visions of grandeur and splendor.

On one hand, simply saying what is on my mind
Does not truth make.
Maybe it is true in my mind,
But the pain that I cause with my Perception of truth
Can be the beginning of my own recession;
Ultimate sadness.

True; I made a commitment to
Oneness, one to honor and obey
My heart and to live in commune with soul
Building where truth's candor
Can reign and fear of judgment's fog
Evaporates into clarity, trust
And a broth of happiness. Drink up.

## Surrender/Humility/Joy Equal: Action, Soul, And Heart.

By RobertEatonSokol

When I was a baby
There was no maybe, when
I'd cry. I knew how I felt.
Life was so simple, and truth
reigned, Cause I had dimples.
"Aw, there, there," mom would say.

When I became a teenager,
All there was, was," maybe,"
Said me, full of confusion and delusions;
Thought my sight was my might,
But I was in for a surprise,
Guised in my ego-to-go.

Then I turned 20 and called Myself a man.
Scanning the horizon, I hid behind elusions
Of power going sour.
I thought babies were cute, but, "love
Meant never having to say you're sorry."

When I turned 30, I thought I understood,
But I had buried real feelings,
Dealing with impressing my soul's depression.
I wondered why relationships
Passed by, filled with conflict.
The edict was, "don't let anyone know
      And I will survive the lie."

I really began growing up when I turned 50.
I got tired of tripping over my own nose;
The dirt was muddy below.
One fine day, I awakened saying, "Enough groveling!"
 I'm mad. I am not going to be sad, another day.
The medicine for my heart was to peel away
The layers of fear that I foolishly used
To protect from life's joys.

Now that I am 60, I understand
What I did and forgot. It seemed,
It is deemed, it is so simple to see the truth,
Without blinders, when fear became absent,
From my view of, in lieu of joy,
 Not a toy of accountability.
Here is the magnet I misplaced,
But which the mirror owned.
I was once so blinded by the glint, that
The hint of truth got lost from my view.

What defines real value,
Is character, not false
Barriers of derrieres,
Truth not ego, joy not fear,
Peace instead of division.
There-in lies real power, this hour.
It is not sour, but is alive and welling
With joy in this dwelling.

Lift up your eyes and see.
Open your ears to soft tears.
Allow your touch to feel.
Taste the nuances of savoring flavor.
Smell the scents others bent for lent.
Release your heart from bondage and
Mend your soul.

## Sweet Heart Of Mine, I Love You
### By RobertEatonSokol

| | |
|---|---|
| **S** | Sweet, describes the |
| **W** | Welling in my heart, |
| **E** | Every time I see your face. |
| **E** | Each time I hear your voice, |
| **T** | Time stands still, just for a moment. |
| **H** | Heavenly is how I feel! |
| **E** | Even when I look away, your |
| **A** | Attention is all I remember. |
| **R** | Ring is what my ears do, |
| **T** | To hear your name, gee wiz and my golly! |
| | |
| **O** | Often, I hear your smile |
| **F** | Foretelling the joy you give. |
| | |
| **M** | My step quickens, |
| **I** | In time with my heart beat. |
| **N** | Never before, have I felt this way, |
| **E**Even in the best of times. | |

I love you, sweet heart of mine, I love you!

# *The Law Of The Candle Light*
## By RobertEatonSokol

Take this light let it shine.
Take this note and let it ring.
Take my blood and let it flow in love.
Take my flesh and let it ring truth.
This is the power you give me.

Then:
Use this power to overcome all doubt.
Use this music to spread the chord of beauty.
Use this love to share my place.
Use your trust to give me strength for
Your re-birth.
Take this power and be great in
Your shadow of humility.

Walk and talk truth; live this power called:

    **Love.**

## *The Mistress Of The Look*
By RobertEatonSokol

You have an "eye" look
That the receiver took
For the lack of words, the Book of Truth
.
Your eyes do the work
Of another's mouth whose
Words cannot really grade your thoughts.

It is your eye brow,
The crooked eye lid that smiled out loud, causing
Other mortals leave open mouthed at your sight.

Curled lips, wrinkled brow
Stops the child cold and
Crops grown folks down low.

You heard me.
I thought I was OK until
I looked at you. The look is your glower power.

Words from my mouth
Are secondary to the power
That comes from your eyes; no lies.

And if I wait a moment longer,
The look will change to something stronger.
The look of love is so soft, supple, with the
Light of fire flies twinkling in your eyes,
       Just waiting for me to say," I am sorry."

## *The Sight Of You Melts Me, You Are Chicken Soup For My Heart*

By RobertEatonSokol

My smile is touched
By your eyes,
Where their love
Knows no lies.

My smile is married
To your curled lips
Which dial-up
The tips of your soul.

My smile is tuned
To your heart
Where visions
Of brain farts lighten mine.

My smile is fixed to you.
Every time I see you,
I feel better and
The world is safer for the rest.

The sight of you,
Melts me.
And I love
Chicken soup too!

# *The Wonderment Of It All*

By RobertEatonSokol

Occasionally in life, I am blessed
with Someone so special that
Exclamations of
Wow, my golly, winks and nods
Are all I can muster in this trumpet call.
 Oh my God,
Said I, the first time I saw your face.
You seemed bigger than
The life surrounding you. You
Were the glue of that held the
room. Oh my God,
Thought I, when I heard your voice
Radiating soft, glowing notes
Knowing the weight, they carried,
Just out of the gate.
Oh my God,
Felt I, as I touched your wrist.
It was the mist that greeted my
delight. The power I thought I had,
melted. Oh my God,
My nostrils reeled at the
scent Of your arrival.
All the pretense of my presence was spent for
Lent. Oh my God,
Felt I as your presence sashayed through the
space. It became my place to claim
A date with this future mate. I am not to
blame. Oh my God and other
Exclamations of remembrances
fill My eyes with joy every day
I awaken in the air you breathe,

My present for not missing the fireworks and fireflies.
Even today, when I see you
In any room, I am surprised
At the wonderment of
All the miles of smiles.
And say, "My, my, my".

## *Valentine's Day And Crazy Love.*
By RoberteatonSokol

In and out, over and about.
When I found it, I was so filled with the noise of joy!

I dream of you,
Morning, noon and night,
Blue or grey skies smile or frown.

I dream of you
Content or not and never down.
I am with you in my heart.

I fell in love with you,
Young or old, as I spied you.
Shy or bold, I dream of you!

When you touched my face,
I entered the race
To find you, so you can touch my love, for you.

You grazed my arm then held my
hand, And my feelings for you
Find this crazy love that is reserved, only, for you.

Happy Valentine's Day.

# Walking By Faith
## By RobertEatonSokol

When I place
Someone above or below,
Love does not flow.

When I peacefully see you
As equal with me
Then love is the only thing that can be.

Walking by faith
Is visible. You can hear it,
You can feel it. It is the truth by which we live.

Living by faith is seeing through love.
It is all the time, awake and asleep.
This is the keeper of our lives.

Faith is the foundation for love,
Before and after lust. It is the food
For growth, the spiritual muscle,
Tussling our hair and the strength in our lives.

# Walking In The Rain
## By RobertEatonSokol

Walking in the rain
Can be such an excellent experience,
Splashing the pavement
As we walk,
Talking through the rain dipping,
Down our chins.
Pings and drips cannot be heard
Because your soft voice is all I hear.

Please read me this poem about
Softly dripping rain peppering
Our faces as we walk.
Your soft voice
Soothes my taste buds so
I can hear you.

When I listen to the sounds,
Of rain, they round out
Words into perfectly formed sounds
And picturesque photographs of
Your composition made of
Winks, blinks, nods and
Sinkers. They are looking for bites.

So here is a sucker.
If I pucker up,
Did you say onion or lemon?
Bunion or seven-up?
Please read your poem

So, I can curl up
Beside you and
Close my eyes in delight
And lose myself in the muses
Of drying out rain drops.

As I lose myself in the soft notes of your voice
I became wrapped in your
Soft rap, rap, rapping,
Like waves lapping
At my awakening views of
you. Your voice is the key to
Soothing my tired mind's eye.

You left me in the closet of your pen.
Please show me a spinner of dreams
And I will look for you, too.

# What Do You Feel?
## By RobertEatonSokol

What do you feel
When you steal
A glance at caring and feeling?

If my eyes
Saw no lies,
Where no one dies,
Then blind would I be
But I saw you instead
And you gave me a couch
To tell this story of glory.

If my nose
Smelled no stink
Where eyes don't blink
Then sad would be me,
But I smelled the roses first
And my eyes twinkled with delight
At the sight that this aroma
Might paint a pallet that would match
Taste with colorful paste.

If my ears
Heard no seared sounds
But sweet mounds, rounded and
Flavored by Beethoven's Fifth
Then happy would describe my mind's
eye; So, my mind rejoices at The
sweetness in tone alone

If my body's senses honored
The sensual tones around it,
It would carve out its delight
In spite of the dusty lust that scratches
Its way, trying to find
A hold in your mold.
But the delight in feeling
The senses leave me daring
To care for this notion of love,
Above, below, inside and out of me!

So, you revel at my slow
hand That finds the best In
the sizzle left by
This carbonated beverage.
Enjoy the moment.
Since my eyes are closed,
My ear creates its own visions
In stereo; you are so beautiful.

If my fingers
Felt no burning
Left by the churning of confusion,
Then the touch is food for delight
That might leave memories from
The sender of sugar plumbs
Dancing in my head because No
touch leaves me sad,
But glad am I that I felt your sins bin.

But the depth of my senses
Would only allow for the music
Left behind by my eyes
Seeing the roses surrounded
By thorns sporting horns.

So, my tongue will heal
This stolen moment in atonement.

If my tongue
Could only taste the paste
Left in haste in the pot,
The sweet spot would have taken a breath
At the depth of sensory delight.
But the depth of my senses
Would only allow for the music
Left behind by my eyes
Seeing the roses surrounded
By thorns sporting horns.
So, my tongue will heal
This stolen moment in atonement.

## *When I Think Of You*
By RobertEatonSokol

When I think of you,
The sun catches your tears and
Wiped them softly away, I say, and
The moon caught your beam so
The stars could shape the sky and sigh,
My, my, my!

 When I know you, I think of majestic peaks
Leaking into meandering streams of dreams.
There are molded boulders and smoldering rocks
Locked into your hills, fairly touching,
Munching the blue mew,
Defining you when you slew my heart.

 As I know you, I see
Valleys of character and
Bushels of heart
Giving me a start! Then,
There are fields of grain,
Wafting their mains and
Strawberries playing peak-a-boo
Through them, giving me
Shivers of delight at your sight!
I love you, too.

# *When Is My House A Home, Not Just On A Clear Day?*
### By RobertEatonSokol

This house is a gift, lifted
From a lack of tone.
Music blows through it
Like a gust of joy.

This house became a home
When a dusty lust for love
Filtered through the open door,
Adding light to the delight of your sight.

The ingredient is a lifting gift,
Sifting through the opened
Curtains, certain that it could
Not be thought of as expedient- a glow
Called love sifted in.

When did this house become a home?
When we walked outside the din; When the
might of sight was declared Humble, not
from a mumble or stumble but Through
declarations and sounders when I found
her, Juanita.

## *You May Be Away*
### By RobertEatonSokol

While you are away
I will not play, but
Stay in my view of you.

While you are not here,
I see your mirror and
Remember how dear your memory is.

And since I cannot touch
Your face, I feel such warmth,
From your missing reflection.

You may be away but the soft tones
Of your voice resonate in my bones.
Your kindness healed my blindness.

In anticipation of your return
I remember how much
I miss you and turn to words of love.

Waiting for your hand to touch mine
Inspires my spirit to view
Mews of your approach. I coach my
heart Where my love for you finds
A place on my tongue when I
proclaim, "Welcome home, my love."
 love you, Happy Valentine's Day."

## Relax And Be Peaceful

By RobertEatonSokol

Let go of control
Seek a bold mole,
The heart of your soul
And this pot of gold.

Surrender to your sender,
The blender of peace within
and Find the splendor of Joyful
Noise with these moments of atonement.

Close your eyes,
And say good-by
To all the lies and
Signs of, "Just trying, I'm buy'n time."

Think kind thoughts of
Bounty, not bought,
But sprinkled from warm or cooling
Breezes, wafting through my trees
In this exercise in relaxation and peace.

Now, give it away.

# *Ain't It Wonderful;*
# *The Color Of Rain?*

By RobertEatonSokol

Life is like love.
It ceases only with the heartbeat.
It starts with a simple cry, full of dependent
adoration. It unravels choices, complete with giving
thanks for Love that loves us back and breaks from
our lips, "hello, to the morning mirror," so dear.

Giving doesn't stop with a minute, an hour or the day, they
say. Giving neither begins at an appointed time of mine,
But grows like the morning glory when the morn adorns
The unexpected song bird atop Mom's clothes line, a sight to dine
on. The gloss of rain, the soft dew or blush of dusk, our Creator
gave us are wonders of the day at bay awaiting soft caresses. It's all
shades of black breathing color to the day, you know.

Trying and failing
Finds the taste and test of faith. Every time we create
A new dish of food, there is a fresh spirit and mood.
Smell and enjoy the aroma and the luxury of good tidings.
Eat and eliminate. Grow a body of faith. This is
The muscle for trust, an asset of the soul without toll.

See good and bad as an essential balance
In the experience of faith building where
A grateful life lived through gratitude is to be joyful.
Happiness is temporary but joy is the fabric of our heart.
I may have been sad, angry, confused or hurt.
Those were events outside my heart and were temporary.
I chose to surrender to Joy and heal my startled heart.
Ain' It wonderful, the color of rain.

# *A Place In My Dreams*
## By RobertEatonSokol

There is a place in my dreams,
Where heaven beams.
It seems things that gleam Are
the views from crystal falls
And turquoise seas where the beaches
Are woven with gold and sand, far as I could see.
Of course, I'm in heaven—guess I died.

There're velvety greens cleansing my feet
And song birds singing their lovely songs to a soft beat.
I'm here. Maybe I'll stay to watch them play.
I see my loved ones, kitties, puppies, too,
Floating on clouds in the skies,
Deep blue—who knew?
No one's crying, just twinkles,
Trying to get my attention.
Not to mention, miles of smiles with
Sweet rainbows stretching style.

I lay down on a marshmallow soft bed,
Where only bunnies dance in my head.
The air is like the sweat breath,
Of forget-me-nots and rose kisses,
My skin and knows no sin.
If this is heaven, then I'm staying.
This is kin to all my dreams.

I see this place in my dreaming space.
I wake up hoping—it is too good
To forget- but think again,
I laugh—nothing on earth but my heart compares to this place.
Perhaps, it came from heaven. If that is where it was from—
above with love, then, I can hardly wait for this date with fate

# *Crazy Love And Beautiful Eyes*
### By RobertEatonSokol

In and out, I shouted, silently.
When I found you,
I was filled with the noise of Joy.
I dreamed of you,
Morning, noon and night—
No fright but Blue skies or grey,
Your sight gave me might.
I dreamed of you.

Content but not spent.
I am with you in my heart, from the start.
I spied you, Young or old;
And fell in love, Shy or bold.
I dream of you; please don't scold.

When you touched my face,
I entered this race to find your heart,
So, you could touch my love, for you.
You grazed my arm, held my hand,
Then touched my neck and my feelings for you,
Found this crazy love.
Yeah, I fell in love with you,
Though you held me at bay, all day.
I'm here to stay.

## Grief And Love Loss
### By RobertEatonSokol

When I love deeply,
I dare to care for another
At a depth that scalds fear,
To see into another's bold soul.
As it suddenly seems to be ripped away,
My heart heats to boiling, unless I turn the heat down.
I must remember that grief and love come from,
Faith and Hope, the ease of these.
When I expect unconditional caring from me to
Thee, I get tenderness in return,
Without asking, basking in the glory of
loves… Sprinkles where ever you've been.
You rescued me, though I was willing, and brought new light.
Thank you, God.
Thank you, God,
Thank you, God. And so, it is.

## *Grief And Love Come From The Same Heart And Loving Soul*

By RobertEatonSokol

Grief sleeps, until it wakes up
At the most unexpected times;
It challenges courage, where we thought
We had some; I implore you to explore more.
To have a heart that never hardens,
That finds goodness where others
See nothing; this is joy, no toy to play with.
And then to suddenly lose the partner-heart, startles the soul.
To have a temperament
That never tries souls, nor asks for tolls, and tells no lies,
But which challenges the ordinary, is a recipe for
goodness. So, there is no confusion in rejoicing with angel
singers, "This joy that I have, the world didn't give it to
me…" To have a touch which never hurts,
But only soothes and asks for help
In understanding, is a gift,
That keeps on giving because,
Grace is a quality not a quantity.
Grief is personal and it is a timeless,
Expression of unimaginable loss,
The depth of which can only be
Born from tender heart tethers of hope and love.

## Go For It, If You Dare

By RobertEatonSokol

If you need an invite,
To get-r-done,
You've lost sight
Of the might in your own delight,
In spite of your mind's view.
If you need courage,
To take action in defining your own
clarity, You've lost sight of the scourge,
Of those detractors who would rob your power
Leaving you sour with no solidarity.
If you think you need permission,
To stand before your conscience,
You have lost your identity
And the serenity that holds in
Your peace of mind, without division.
Think and then," Go for it."

## *Last Time I Knew*
### By RobertEatonSokol

Whispers, where poems live
Just waiting to give
Power to a tower of words,
Expressions of truth that live
Where birds
Fly my sky, disguised as wind.
Last time I knew, these were words I give.
I have dreams of playing
In the grass with my lassie,
Watching the willowy sky
Where all nature's creatures fly
And wave my, my, by, by,
As they give residence to birds and bees with
wings And other things that also land in the sand
With the falling dew at
Curfew above this rising mud with a thud.
What I face is beyond your lazy smile
And titling wit and keeps my attention,
As we make our way
To meet for our heavenly, Loving
date of delight in spite of Falling
battle hymns of directed notes and
the sky's tear drops.
I'm really not thirsty for more of this lore's score.
Too loud for me to me here more.

# *Hurry, Time's Old...*
## By RobertEatonSokol

"Hurry, hurry," said the wind,
"Day is slipping 'round the bend.
I can't wait another minute. Find it and send it.
I know I need to have you in it, this time."

"Hurry, hurry," said the sun.
"Soon the day'll be done.
I can't leave you in the dark.
You'll need the sun to light your spark in your park."

"Hurry, hurry," said the Lune's moon.
"I'll see you very soon.
Don't let this day pass by and by. For
soon, I'll claim the sky-good-by."

"Hurry, hurry," said Father/Mother Time, "I
steal minutes, but that's no crime," I sigh.
"'Taint no lie. Let's make a deal," I said with a wily smile.

"I need you here. Please stay a while?"
"So, pileup those wishes and dishes,
Of love so I can shove them into warm ovens and
Pockets of wondrous dreams, seal these deals and
other gloves to save them for good times and beaming dreams."

# Lonely One
## By RoberteatonSokol

One yellow daffodil,
Crown on its head,
Standing tall and perfectly still, not
dead, On this lonesome hill,
Facing all odds, on this window sill.
One yellow daffodil,
All alone, at least until
Others fill the hill, so,
Mom can harvest them for the sill.
The ravished beds of winter-kills,
Bulbs fill, sending them, thrilling us.
One yellow daffodil, no longer
Shivering, alone in nature's chill.
Not quite sure what the deal is,
That leaves her alone on the hill.
Mom's eagle eye watches, catches glimpses of life
And her knife, to save this glory for this story.
One daffodil,
I can relate to how you felt?
As I, too, braved that house on the wondrous hill.
What a thrill.

# *I Will Be. I Am.*

### By RobertEatonSokol

Where ever love leads me
I will go. Say, "Yes," to forgiving hearts,
And, "No," to tolled anger tarts.
Faith is the courage of my intention.
I go there and find acceptance, not
Loose perceptions of false barriers.
Where there is strength behind my words,
I am there and find real life discernment,
And integrity where truth builds heart muscles, and song birds

As I find my strength to chart my own course,

I see beyond my horizon, dearth, lack and limitation.
There I find the rebirth of my soul.
The directions I go, find
I am that I am, where
There is no pain or fear, so kind to some there.
When I am open to Love,
I lead quietly and leave my past un-forgiveness
To the power of receiving love goals, here and above other souls.

Change is power, knocking down walls of division,
Releasing clouds of ignorance and derision,
Giving me permission to see love's power, clearly.
I do not require permission to be willing.
I will be there, for you and me,
Too.

## Snow Move Over· Shovels Are Here With Cheer-Wind Has Died Down

By RobertEatonSokol

Its snow-covered sidewalks,
Yet again, through Winters evening, I
believe. This frisky cold reminds me not to
leave and To put on extra sleeves. Silence
bores the night,
As snow scores another sifter down.
Wrapped round baby, tucked in instead.
We're dressed up in sleeping gowns to drowned
Out cold, while trying to bury cracks in doors, I'm
told. The porch light shines down steps
And across the yard, adding glimmers to
The cars- parked in the shimmering dark.
Snuggling in front of our fireplace,
We're toasty in front of this dreamed-of glow.
Flames are low, to go where dreams sew
Streams of lit fantasies.
Perhaps Spring has lost its way…
It stays away a bit longer. It's taking it's time.
It's old you know.
We're ok with snow leftovers,
It's just us, our fake fireplace and spirits of
wine, To dine on.

## *We Are*

By RobertEatonSokol

We are alone, together,
Though living worlds apart.
We are alone together,
We share a broken heart.
Is this the stuff poets' use?
Does suffering birth the most prolific muse?
Let's not so easily dismiss,
The power of verse and rhyme.
What I mean to say is this:
Suffering sculpts the best design.
Let's use the past as kindling
To build a crackling fire.
We'll talk all night of dreams deferred,
About our shared desire.
When we finally fall asleep
With the promise of a kiss,
We'll wake to find a bridge across
That deep and wide abyss,
Where all regrets and sense of loss,
And thorny fear will dismiss.
When all broken pieces meld
Into one heart, beating strong,
It will withstand the truth of the day,
Fielding questions all night long.
It will beat a sure and steady rhythm,
And make two something new, forever.
How strange this algorithm,
That keeps two together
And makes us one, not two apart.

One hope, one dream, one beating heart.
Until the very last note
Of our love song is finished,
Itself the final lyric wrote.
The very last chord is now diminished.
The last breath, a promissory note,
Unpaid until the last reframe.
Our story stored in anecdote.
Yet softest whispers still remain,
The distant echo of the lover's song,
For those who know what sorrow
teaches; To love—is never wrong.

## *Time's Up, O''L Girl, You Wore Me Out And I'm Almost Dead.*
By RobertEatonSokol

Don't pack your lies in my place,
Or search for a corner in my space,
In case you planned on a longer stay to play.
Don't stand there and tell me, to my face, that
I can smell your lace, that the sky is blue,
When it's obviously grey. Please stay but,
Don't tell me you love me and then walk away.
Don't stack your flap-jacks on my plate
Waiting for butter and maple syrup, then
Leave at dawn, saying you're running late,
For another date. I've had my fill of half-full
Coffee cups- just sip your tea, please. By the way,
Your wig is up?
Don't leave your boots 'beneath my bed.
Don't make up words I wish you'd said instead.
Just plant your feet on the floor
And follow your shadow out the door, some more.
Don't leave a tip or any lip, just toss a kiss
As you go out the door.
Your time's up,
Come back no more, I'm sore.

## *Sweet Temptations, Married To Me*

By RobertEatonSokol

I've got peppermint in my hand.
A rushing feeling, I cannot stand.
The urge for her chocolate chunks and
crunch, Cookies is just too great.
Easily, I lose control. It's too darned late!
Her cupboard gate beacons.
I have hot tea leaves
Up my sleeve and in my cup
And it's time to sip up.
This day has caught me way too fast
And I hope these urges soon will pass, alas.
Now one of her chunky cookies looks at me.
It found my hand. I don't know how?
It looks quite tempting from where I
stand, Just minding my own business.
The cookie jar's just too close, mostly…
I just need another dose of her mesmerizing chunks
Of chocolate and peppermint to leave a dent.
If I don't hurry and leave this place,
No morsels will be left, leaving me bereft of my dripping
tongue. Not one crumb!!!Not a trace!!!!
And I'll be waddling out the door
Wishing for more, then sauntering
back, 'til there's none for lore…

## *Spring Break*

By RobertEatonSokol

A blanket of white before me,
As snow claims another day,
To bay for the wind calming, trees sway.
Spring will begin its invasion
While keeping winter at bay.
An eerie sense of defilement
Sounds this pending day.
Winter has worn out it's stay
But refuses to step away.
Pine tree limbs sag,
Covered heavy with snow.
I sit, watching its misery
Wishing winter would just go.
I feel a sense of peace and calm.
Not one bit of noise, He/She makes.
Winter wants more attention.
Spring can't catch a break. It
may take a miracle for
Nature to grant this wish and
A dish of chocolate pudding and
milk, To take

## About the Author

Robert Eaton Sokol is a true Renaissance man. Heart Poet, wood sculptor, and Award-Winning new home and renovation designer. He blends his passion for life and people in everything he does. This second addition collection of poetry and prose is a sample of the bounty and journey of self-discovery. It is dedicated to all those who chose to," Celebrate Life," and all its riches.

Peace and Blessings,

Robert Eaton Sokol

www.ingramcontent.com/pod-product-compliance
Lightning Source LLC
Chambersburg PA
CBHW030528080526
44586CB00011B/362